an unlikely conversation

a student and teacher bridge a 50-year age span

Mary Anker & Will Grant

an unlikely conversation

Copyright 2021 by Mary Anker and Will Grant
All rights reserved.

Cover art by Emma Sattler
Copyright 2021

Interior art by Elsa Grant
Copyright 2021

ISBN: 978-1-950381-88-3

Published by Piscataqua Press
An imprint of RiverRun Bookstore, Inc
32 Daniel St., Portsmouth NH 03801

www.ppressbooks.com

Printed in the United States

INTRO

Ten years ago I walked into Mary's 7th grade English class at Berwick Academy for the first time. I chose a desk in the back corner as I always did and waited anxiously for class to begin. I was immediately intimidated by her. She spoke like she meant business and demanded respect just by walking into the room. I slumped back into my chair thinking to myself that it was going to be a long year.

Being a well-versed poet herself, Mary assigned many poetry assignments to our class over the course of the year. Poetry was something I had never really tried before. To my surprise, I took a great liking to it. It was a creative freedom I was finding for the first time. I wrote many poems in her class, but the pinnacle of my poetic career that year came when Mary pulled me aside one day in the spring and asked me if I would read one of my poems in a poetry reading at Portsmouth's RiverRun Bookstore the following week. Astonished but delighted, I accepted. As I read my poem in front of a jam-packed audience that day, I realized that Mary had given me confidence like no other teacher had before. She felt like my biggest fan.

After middle school it was a few years before Mary and I re-connected. I suppose the excitement and drama of high school had carried me away for a while. It wasn't until sometime after my senior year in high school that we decided to email each other. Our emails with the added poems were sporadic, but they were a thread. I also shared my song lyrics. Six years later, after I graduated and was working in Boston, Mary recommended I read a poetry book called *Braided Creek: A Conversation in Poetry* by Ted Kooser and Jim Harrison. It was a book of communication written via short poems between two poets over time. Mary suggested we put our poems in a book ourselves. This book is that conversation of poems. It captures our individual yet intertwined journeys of thought over the years — from college life to grandchildren and everywhere in between.

This book has both allowed us and forced us to keep in touch. It has fostered a relationship that is unique. For that I am ever grateful. I hope you enjoy our book.

DEEP APPRECIATION

Emma Sattler created the print for the cover of *an unlikely conversation*. We thank her for those unmoored windows. They catch the winds of time and our wandering lines of communication.

Emma is a 2021 graduate of Massachusetts College of Art and Design, with a BFA in Printmaking.

Elsa Grant designed the interior artwork that marks six calendar years. We appreciate how closely she read our poems and for her bold yet nuanced visual response to them.

Elsa is a 2021 graduate of the University of Southern California with a BFA in Design.

2016

looking at a withered leaf
wander the street
with barely a wind
my heart beats faster

a yellow leaf dangles
I want to glue it
to the gray tree
it falls though
I forget about it

my shoes have holes
wide enough for time
to pass through
unnoticed

on a pallet skyward
blue stretches
so thin
it snaps and cracks time
we slide inside

books whisper
their unread secrets
on a dusty shelf
craving the touch
of a college student

it was not frigid
but we were hungry
the two of us
and that made us
colder

2017

lunch across a small table
shrinks the fifty-year gap

errands with my 7th grade English teacher
oddly I enjoyed it

staring out a window all day
until dad comes home
this dog's life

awake in a sleeping neighborhood
coughing thick pollen
a sudden zip of a motorbike
startles the scissors scratching her back

she passes me on the sidewalk
her cheap perfume
I am 13 again
naive at a middle school dance

on my bike
racing
cutting across the parking lot
August 1955
and
August 2017

stuck between then and now
those wavelengths and that bandwidth
needed
to dance in the dark

tried to slow down
the day
by watching the sunset

Trying not to sleep
On my youth
It's whirling by

waiting for a wave
floating in the horizon
it finally appears
first the smooth curve
then the crash and long scrape

2018

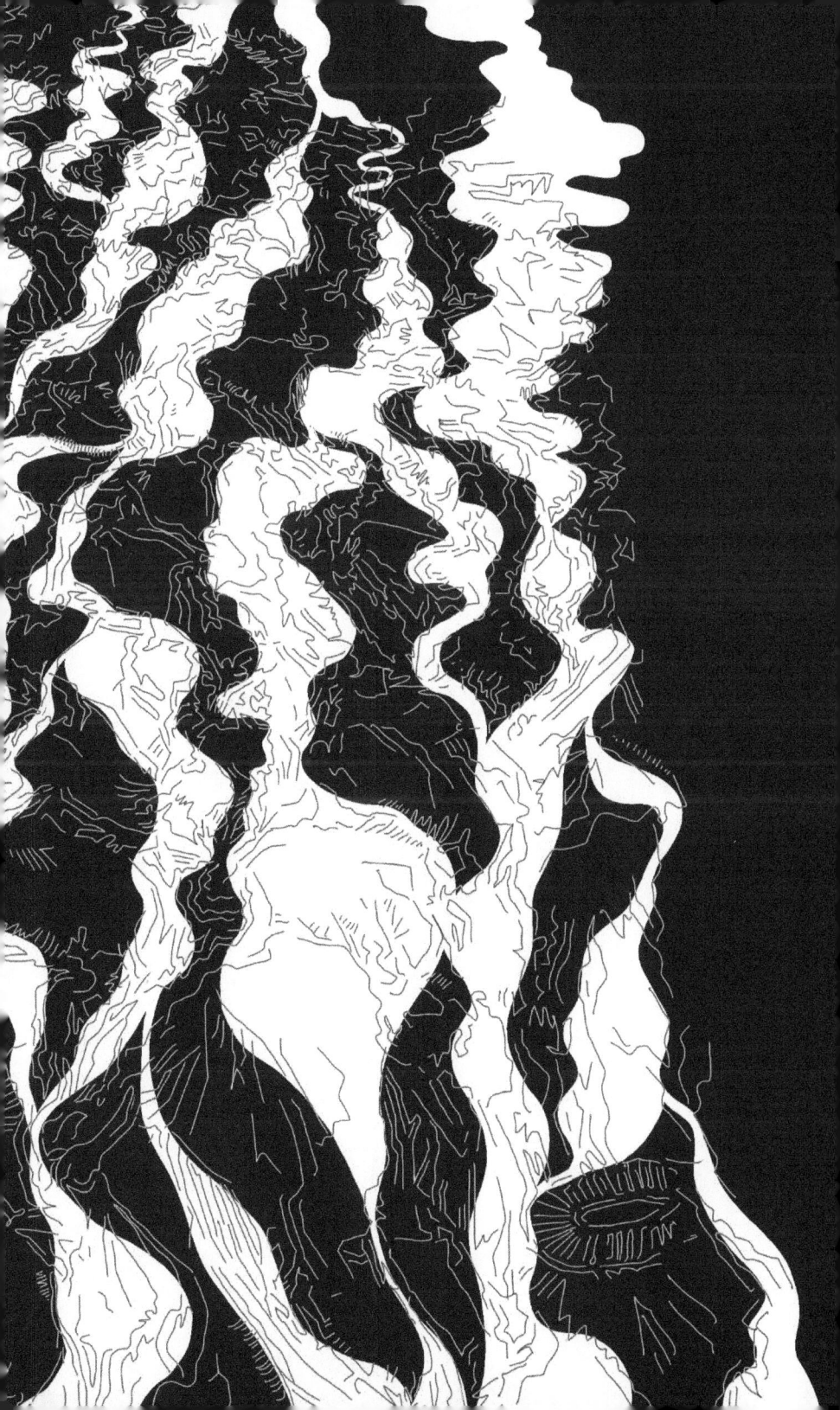

Adult?
Is it me?
Am I the one I imagined?
When I was three?

The trick:
Use your inside
image
to paint your
outside reality.

the convenience of my phone
leaves me alone
scrolling in my bed
with memories unmade

wishing for the past
no cell phones
untethered
closer to one another

arriving in the future
singing a song from the past
I tripped over you

A twisting in my stomach
For the first time in a while
That's how I know I like you

time used to be a languid river
now it is a freeway
eight lanes blurring by
as I hold out my thumb for a ride

bullshitted essay gets a 3.75
cocktail party king
these drunken dreams
college, don't leave me

2019

my grandson read my spirit
card today, a hyena's message:
*What would happen if you took
your goals seriously?*

These beautiful days
we will think about
years from now
the scarlet and the brown
on the campus of our dreams

foreign places
we find ourselves
Home

waking up
to senior spring sun
finally I have
an old lover's eyes

no matter
the freezing of lips
the feels like -7 temp
shooting baskets with him
maybe my last chance

I'll remember
these sleepless nights
swimming in the wave of sheets
dancing till dawn with you

love
his decision
his life for hers

this corporate game
of hitting quotas
fuels me
for now

he skims up the tree
no bother to the new nest
dances shirtless on top of the shed
his wings beating

grant your
wild self
a deep & secret wilderness
live there
with the path open

some kind of relentless truth
seeks me
as I lie awake
at night
dreaming

in an instant
fall
a new season
how long
how far
how tenuous
an instant?

to revise my eyes
I stumble
struggling
to lighten the load
on the way

United Nations 2019
dark-windowed black Suburban diplomacy
unsmiling men   stiletto women
teetering

At 4:30 am
We take a walk in the park
Over the Oakland bridge
And we glide

Berkeley, CA 1962
vocabulary over my head
subsequently
enlightening

remember
Emily's
Dwell in Possibility

2020

Gin and Jam
Boston Creme
Wood paneled hubbub
Next phase

Coffee
Mint chocolate chip ice cream
Backgammon
In the sun
For breakfast

In the forest thick
Wind, a companion, nodding
Our ascent to blue

2021

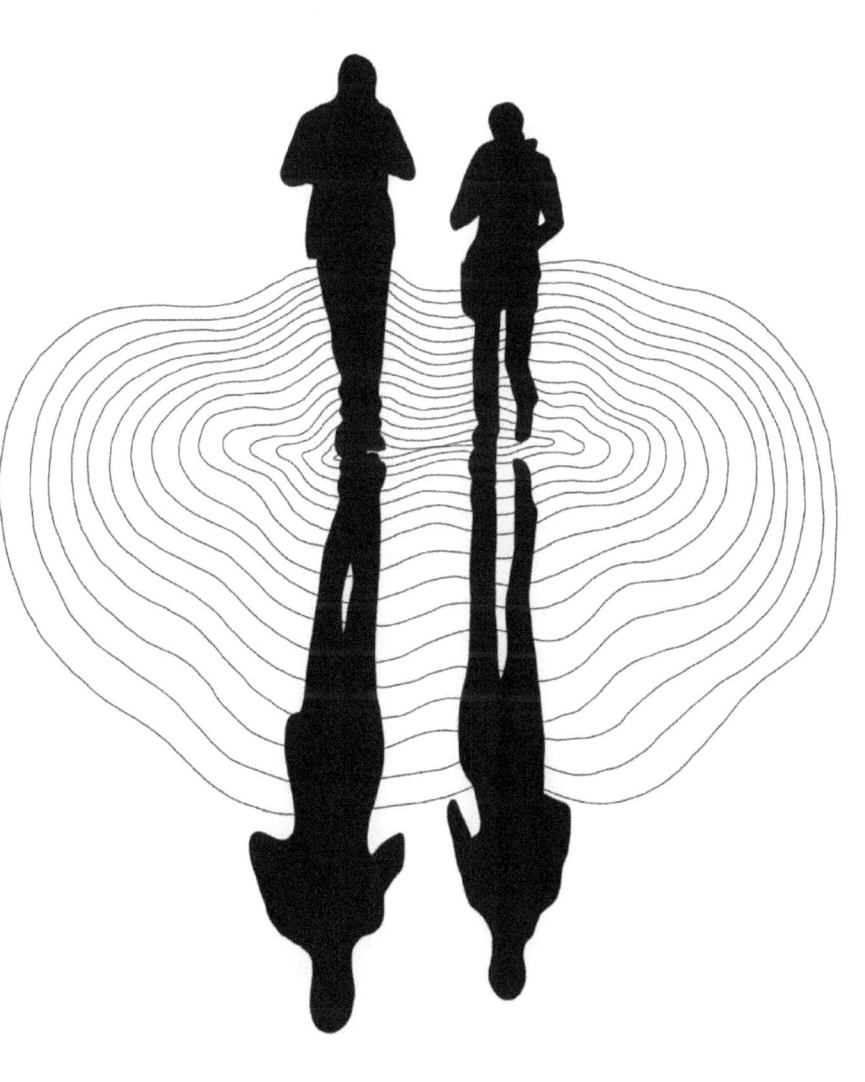

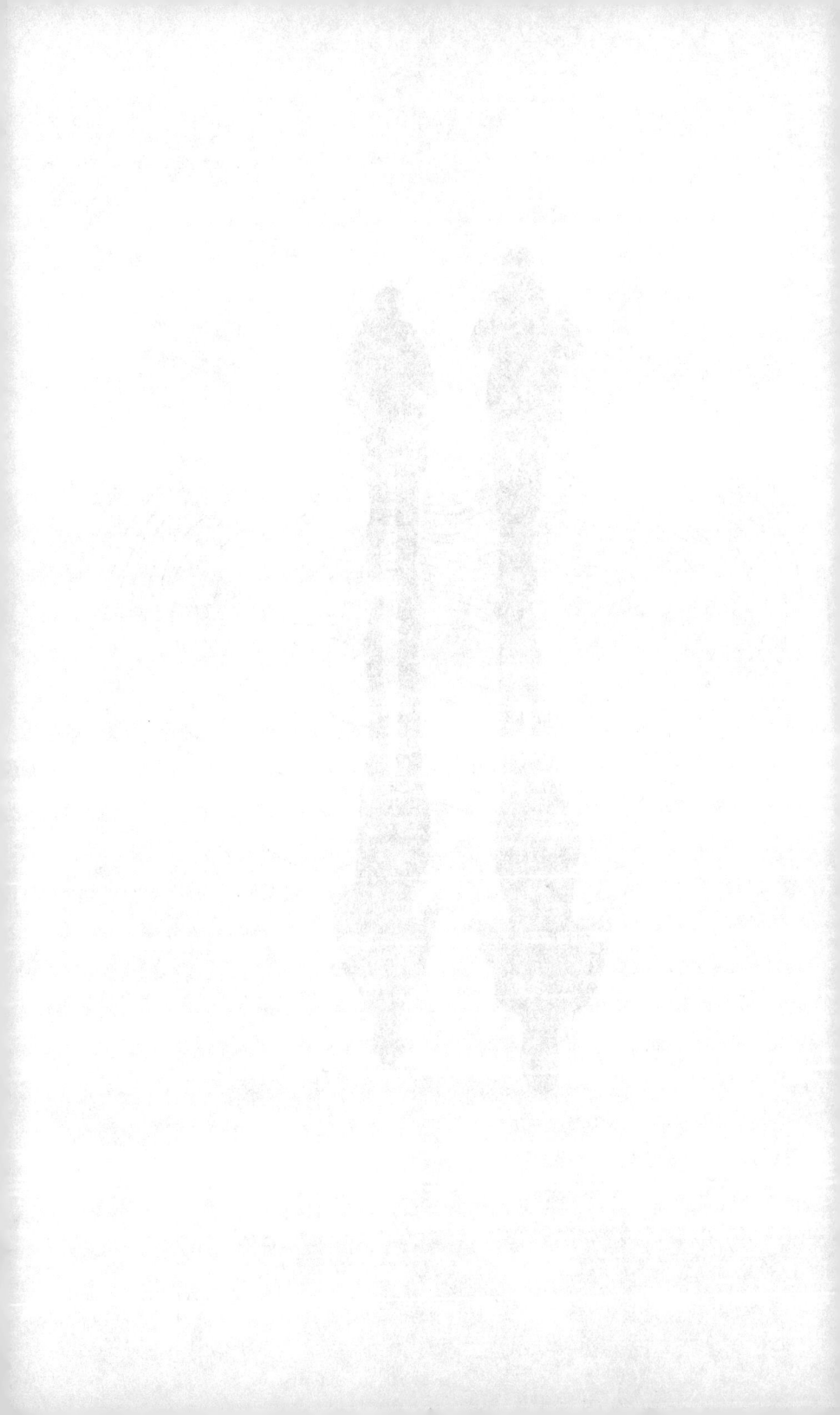

careening dreams
red-tailed hawk
wild descent screams
mostly in the mind now
still as air in high pines
watching
for the slightest wind

a twist in fate
the T thunders through
barbaric and cold
wake me, golden morning
that warmth of a new day
I'm ready
for now

Mary Anker started teaching English in 1968 in Portland, Oregon and has taught in NYC, New Hampshire, and Maine. In the early 2000s, she began presenting her poetry at local readings. Her poetry has appeared in several anthologies. Two poems, *I, Too, Sing the Piscataqua* and *Cancer Creations* won awards. She is the co-founder of the Mary Anker Poet-in-Residence series at Berwick Academy. She lives in Portsmouth, New Hampshire with her husband and travels regularly to San Francisco and New York to be with grandchildren.

Will Grant grew up in the small beach town of Rye, New Hampshire, yet he has regrettably still not learned how to surf. He started writing poetry in 7th grade, and through encouragement of his English teachers, would go on to win poetry competitions and give poetry readings at local venues like The River Run Bookstore and The Press Room. A philosophy major in college, Will's poetry evolved into lyric and song writing as his passion for music began to flourish. The dozens of songs that Will has written and produced can be found on Soundcloud under his artist name, WILL YG. At the age of 24, Will currently lives in New York City where he works as an account executive for a tech company. He spends his evenings bar hopping, going to indie rock concerts, and playing too much chess. *an unlikely conversation* is Will's first published poetry book, and he is honored to have written it with his mentor and longtime friend, Mary Anker.

www.ingramcontent.com/pod-product-compliance
Lightning Source LLC
Chambersburg PA
CBHW032103040426
42449CB00007B/1165